by Iain Gray

Lang Syne

PUBLISHING

WRITING *to* REMEMBER

LangSyne
PUBLISHING
WRITING *to* REMEMBER

E-mail: info@lang-syne.co.uk

Distributed in the Republic of Ireland by Portfolio Group,
Kilbarrack Ind. Est. Kilbarrack, Dublin 5.
T:00353(01) 839 4918 F:00353(01) 839 5826
sales@portfoliogroup.ie
www.portfoliogroup.ie

Design by Dorothy Meikle   Printed by Ricoh Print Scotland

© Lang Syne Publishers Ltd 2012

ISBN 978-1-85217-411-8

O'Neill

MOTTO:
Lám Dearg Éirinn
(The Red Hand of Ireland).

CREST:
An arm in armour clutching a sword.

NAME variations include:
MacNeil
MacNeal
MacNeill
Neill
O'Neal
O'Neall
O'Neil
Uí Néill *(Gaelic)*

Chapter one:
Origins of Irish surnames

**According to an old saying, there are two types of Irish –
those who actually are Irish and those who wish they were.**

This sentiment is only one example of the allure that the
high romance and drama of the proud nation's history holds
for thousands of people scattered across the world today.

It's a sad fact, however, that the vast majority of Irish
surnames are found far beyond Irish shores, rather than on
the Emerald Isle itself.

The population stood at around eight million souls in
1841, but today it stands at fewer than six million.

This is mainly a tragic consequence of the potato
famine, also known as the Great Hunger, which devastated
Ireland between 1845 and 1849.

The Irish peasantry had become almost wholly reliant
for basic sustenance on the potato, first introduced from the
Americas in the seventeenth century.

When the crop was hit by a blight, at least 800,000
people starved to death while an estimated two million
others were forced to seek a new life far from their native
shores – particularly in America, Canada, and Australia.

The effects of the potato blight continued until about
1851, by which time a firm pattern of emigration had
become established.

Ireland's loss, however, was to the gain of the countries in which the immigrants settled, contributing enormously, as their descendants do today, to the well being of the nations in which their forefathers settled.

But those who were forced through dire circumstance to establish a new life in foreign parts never forgot their roots, or the proud heritage and traditions of the land that gave them birth.

Nor do their descendants.

It is a heritage that is inextricably bound up in the colourful variety of Irish names themselves – and the origin and history of these names forms an integral part of the vibrant drama that is the nation's history, one of both glorious fortune and tragic misfortune.

This history is well documented, and one of the most important and fascinating of the earliest sources are *The Annals of the Four Masters*, compiled between 1632 and 1636 by four friars at the Franciscan Monastery in County Donegal.

Compiled from earlier sources, and purporting to go back to the Biblical Deluge, much of the material takes in the mythological origins and history of Ireland and the Irish.

This includes tales of successive waves of invaders and settlers such as the Fomorians, the Partholonians, the Nemedians, the Fir Bolgs, the Tuatha De Danann, and the Laigain.

Of particular interest are the *Milesian Genealogies*,

because the majority of Irish clans today claim a descent from either Heremon, Ir, or Heber – three of the sons of Milesius, a king of what is now modern day Spain.

These sons invaded Ireland in the second millennium B.C, apparently in fulfilment of a mysterious prophecy received by their father.

This Milesian lineage is said to have ruled Ireland for nearly 3,000 years, until the island came under the sway of England's King Henry II in 1171 following what is known as the Cambro-Norman invasion.

This is an important date not only in Irish history in general, but for the effect the invasion subsequently had for Irish surnames.

'Cambro' comes from the Welsh, and 'Cambro-Norman' describes those Welsh knights of Norman origin who invaded Ireland.

But they were invaders who stayed, inter-marrying with the native Irish population and founding their own proud dynasties that bore Cambro-Norman names such as Archer, Barbour, Brannagh, Fitzgerald, Fitzgibbon, Fleming, Joyce, Plunkett, and Walsh – to name only a few.

These 'Cambro-Norman' surnames that still flourish throughout the world today form one of the three main categories in which Irish names can be placed – those of Gaelic-Irish, Cambro-Norman, and Anglo-Irish.

Previous to the Cambro-Norman invasion of the twelfth century, and throughout the earlier invasions and settlement of those wild bands of sea rovers known as the Vikings in the eighth and ninth centuries, the population of the island was relatively small, and it was normal for a person to be identified through the use of only a forename.

But as population gradually increased and there were many more people with the same forename, surnames were adopted to distinguish one person, or one community, from another.

Individuals identified themselves with their own particular tribe, or 'tuath', and this tribe – that also became known as a clann, or clan – took its name from some distinguished ancestor who had founded the clan.

The Gaelic-Irish form of the name Kelly, for example, is Ó Ceallaigh, or O'Kelly, indicating descent from an original 'Ceallaigh', with the 'O' denoting 'grandson of.' The name was later anglicised to Kelly.

The prefix 'Mac' or 'Mc', meanwhile, as with the clans of the Scottish Highlands, denotes 'son of.'

Although the Irish clans had much in common with their Scottish counterparts, one important difference lies in what are known as 'septs', or branches, of the clan.

Septs of Scottish clans were groups who often bore an entirely different name from the clan name but were under the clan's protection.

In Ireland, septs were groups that shared the same name and who could be found scattered throughout the four provinces of Ulster, Leinster, Munster, and Connacht.

The 'golden age' of the Gaelic-Irish clans, infused as their veins were with the blood of Celts, pre-dates the Viking invasions of the eighth and ninth centuries and the Norman invasion of the twelfth century, and the sacred heart of the country was the Hill of Tara, near the River Boyne, in County Meath.

Known in Gaelic as 'Teamhar na Rí', or Hill of Kings, it was the royal seat of the 'Ard Rí Éireann', or High King of Ireland, to whom the petty kings, or chieftains, from the island's provinces were ultimately subordinate.

It was on the Hill of Tara, beside a stone pillar known as the Irish 'Lia Fáil', or Stone of Destiny, that the High Kings were inaugurated and, according to legend, this stone would emit a piercing screech that could be heard all over Ireland when touched by the hand of the rightful king.

The Hill of Tara is today one of the island's main tourist attractions.

Opposition to English rule over Ireland, established in the wake of the Cambro-Norman invasion, broke out frequently and the harsh solution adopted by the powerful forces of the Crown was to forcibly evict the native Irish from their lands.

These lands were then granted to Protestant colonists, or 'planters', from Britain.

Many of these colonists, ironically, came from Scotland and were the descendants of the original 'Scotti', or 'Scots', who gave their name to Scotland after migrating there in the fifth century A.D., from the north of Ireland.

Colonisation entailed harsh penal laws being imposed on the majority of the native Irish population, stripping them practically of all of their rights.

The Crown's main bastion in Ireland was Dublin and its environs, known as the Pale, and it was the dispossessed peasantry who lived outside this Pale, desperately striving to eke out a meagre living.

It was this that gave rise to the modern-day expression of someone or something being 'beyond the pale'.

Attempts were made to stamp out all aspects of the ancient Gaelic-Irish culture, to the extent that even to bear a Gaelic-Irish name was to invite discrimination.

This is why many Gaelic-Irish names were anglicised with, for example, and noted above, Ó Ceallaigh, or O'Kelly, being anglicised to Kelly.

Succeeding centuries have seen strong revivals of Gaelic-Irish consciousness, however, and this has led to many families reverting back to the original form of their name, while the language itself is frequently found on the fluent tongues of an estimated 90,000 to 145,000 of the island's population.

Ireland's turbulent history of religious and political strife is one that lasted well into the twentieth century, a landmark century that saw the partition of the island into the twenty-six counties of the independent Republic of

Ireland, or Eire, and the six counties of Northern Ireland, or Ulster.

Dublin, originally founded by Vikings, is now a vibrant and truly cosmopolitan city while the proud city of Belfast is one of the jewels in the crown of Ulster.

It was Saint Patrick who first brought the light of Christianity to Ireland in the fifth century A.D.

Interpretations of this Christian message have varied over the centuries, often leading to bitter sectarian conflict – but the many intricately sculpted Celtic Crosses found all over the island are symbolic of a unity that crosses the sectarian divide.

It is an image that fuses the 'old gods' of the Celts with Christianity.

All the signs from the early years of this new millennium indicate that sectarian strife may soon become a thing of the past – with the Irish and their many kinsfolk across the world, be they Protestant or Catholic, finding common purpose in the rich tapestry of their shared heritage.

Chapter two:

Royal and ancient

Derived from the original personal forename 'Niall', indicating 'champion' or 'passionate', O'Neill and its many spelling variants is a surname with roots that lie deep in the ancient soil of Ireland.

So deep are these roots that the O'Neills of today are recognised as having one of the world's oldest and most illustrious pedigrees – one that stretches so back through the dim mists of time that historical fact becomes colourfully and dramatically entwined in myth and legend.

In common with other native Irish clans, the O'Neills trace a descent from one of the sons of Milesius, a king of what is now modern day Spain, and who had planned to invade Ireland in fulfilment of a mysterious Druidic prophecy.

Milesius died before he could launch his invasion across the sea to Ireland, but eight sons who included Amergin, Hebor, Ir and Heremon undertook the task.

Five sons, including Ir, were killed in battle against the Tuatha-De-Danann shortly after battling their way from the shoreline to the soil of Ireland.

This was soil, however, that Ir's offspring and the offspring of his brothers Heber and Heremon were destined to hold for centuries as warrior kings.

According to the Milesian genealogies, Heremon and

Heber began to rule the land they had conquered from about 1699 B.C.

The O'Neills trace a descent from Heremon, who killed both Amergin and Heber in quarrels over territory.

The central motif of the Coat of Arms for the various branches of what became the dynasty of the Royal House of O'Neill all feature the famed Red Hand of Ireland – a red hand with the palm facing outwards – while the clan motto is Lám Dearg Éirinn, the Irish Gaelic for Red Hand of Ireland.

One legend holds that this came about when, as their invading ancestors were approaching the extreme northern tip of Ireland, it was agreed that the one who landed first would be granted that particular area of land.

One quick-thinking warrior took his battle-axe and chopped off one of his hands, then threw it with all his might onto the shore – thus claiming the land.

In keeping with their illustrious and royal roots, it is from Niall Noíghiallach, better known to posterity as the great fourth century warrior king Niall of the Nine Hostages, that the O'Neills also claim a descent.

The dramatic life and times of this ancestor of the O'Neills are steeped in stirring Celtic myth and legend.

The youngest son of a king of the province of Connacht, his mother died in childbirth and he was brought up by his evil stepmother Mongfhinn who, to further her own dynastic ambitions, was determined that he should die.

She abandoned him naked on the Hill of Tara, inauguration site of the Ard Rí, or High Kings, of Ireland, but a wandering bard found him and took him back to his father.

One legend is that the king sent Niall and his four brothers to a renowned prophet who was also a blacksmith to determine which of them would succeed their father as Ard Rí.

The blacksmith, known as Sitchin, set the lads a task by deliberately setting fire to his forge.

Niall's brothers ran in and came out carrying the spearheads, fuel, hammers and barrels of beer that they had rescued, but Niall staggered out clutching the heavy anvil so vital to the blacksmith's trade.

By this deed, Sitchin prophesied that Niall would be the one who would take on the glorious mantle of kingship.

Another prophetic incident occurred one day while Niall and his brothers were engaged in the hunt.

Thirsty from their efforts they encountered an ugly old woman who offered them water – but only in return for a kiss.

Three of the lads, no doubt repelled by her green teeth and scaly skin, refused. One brother pecked her lightly on the cheek and, by this act, she prophesied that he would one day reign at Tara – but only briefly.

The bold Niall, however, kissed her fully on the lips. The hag then demanded that he should now have full sexual intercourse with her and, undaunted, he did so.

Through this action she was suddenly transformed into

a stunningly beautiful young woman known as Flaithius, or Royalty, who predicted that he would become the greatest High King of Ireland.

His stepmother later tried to poison him, but accidentally took the deadly potion herself and died.

Niall became Ard Rí in 379 A.D. and embarked on the series of military campaigns and other daring adventures that would subsequently earn him the title of Niall of the Nine Hostages.

The nine countries and territories into which he raided and took hostages for ransom were the Irish provinces of Munster, Leinster, Connacht, and Ulster, Britain, and the territories of the Saxons, Morini, Picts and Dalriads.

Niall's most famous hostage was a young lad known as Succat, son of Calpernius, a Romano-Briton who lived in the area of present day Milford Haven, on the Welsh coast.

Later known as Patricius, or Patrick, he became renowned as Ireland's patron saint, St. Patrick, responsible for bringing the light of Christianity to the island in the early years of the fifth century A.D.

Raiding in Gaul, in the area of Boulogne-sur-mer in present day France, Niall was ambushed and killed by one of his treacherous subjects in 405 A.D.

Niall's legacy is that he was the founder of the royal and mighty dynasty of Uí Néill – 'descendants of Niall.'

This was through seven of his sons, who included Eóghan, founder of the Cenél nEógain dynasty.

One of Eóghan's descendants was Niall Glandubh – Niall of the Black Knee – a late ninth century High King at Tara whose grandson, Domhnall, was the first to assume the surname of Niall, or O'Neill.

The O'Neills became established throughout the Emerald Isle in groupings known as the Northern Uí Néill and the Southern Uí Néill, with the former achieving and maintaining for centuries particular dominance in the province of Ulster.

It was Niall's son, Eóghan, for example, who gave his name to Tir Eóghain, better known today as Northern Ireland's County Tyrone.

The O'Neills of Tyrone became the pre-eminent branch of the O'Neills, other distinguished branches of which include the Clanaboy O'Neills, of Co. Antrim, and the O'Neills of the Fews, of Co. Armagh.

It was the O'Neills of Tyrone whose chiefs were recognised as 'The O'Neill Mór', or 'The Great O'Neill' – a title that has survived to this day through an unbroken descent through the male line.

At the time of writing, there are plans by an umbrella group of international O'Neill clan organisations to establish a library and museum in Ulster dedicated to the clan's proud history.

Chapter three:
Rebellion and exile

What subsequently proved to be the death knell of the rich and vibrant Gaelic way of life of native Irish clans such as the O'Neills was sounded in May of 1169, when the first in a wave of battle-hardened Norman barons, knights and their retainers crossed the sea from Wales and landed at Bannow, in Co. Wexford.

So fierce and disciplined was their onslaught on the forces of the native Irish that by 1171 they had captured Dublin and other strategically important territories.

In that same year, England's Henry II landed on the island to receive the homage and allegiance of his Norman barons in return for their holding the territories they had conquered in the king's name.

Henry also received the submission and homage of many of the Irish chieftains, with English dominion over Ireland ratified through the Treaty of Windsor of 1175.

While many native Irish had to reluctantly bend with the chill winds of the time and seek an accommodation with the powerful forces of the English Crown, the O'Neills proved notably resilient in resisting encroachments onto their Ulster territories.

Rebellion was frequent, particularly over the policy known as 'plantation', or settlement of loyal Protestants on lands previously held by the native Irish.

Rebellion erupted in 1594 against the increasingly harsh treatment of the native Irish and at its forefront were the great Hugh O'Neill, 2nd Earl of Tyrone, and the O'Donnell chieftain Red Hugh O'Donnell.

In what became known as *Cogadh na Naoi mBliama*, or the Nine Years War, the forces of O'Neill and O'Donnell literally set the island ablaze in a vicious campaign of guerrilla warfare.

They inflicted a defeat on an English army at the battle of Clontibert in 1596, while in August of 1598 another significant defeat was inflicted at the battle of Yellow Ford.

As English control over Ireland teetered on the brink of collapse, thousands of more troops, including mercenaries, were hastily despatched to the island and, in the face of the overwhelming odds against them, O'Neill and O'Donnell sought help from England's enemy, Spain.

A well-equipped Spanish army under General del Aquila landed at Kinsale in December of 1601, but was forced into surrender only a few weeks later, in January of 1602.

Resistance continued until 1603, but proved abortive.

Three years later, in September of 1607 and in what is still lamented to this day as The Flight of the Earls, Hugh O'Neill and Rory O'Donnell, 1st Earl of Tyrconnel, sailed into foreign exile from the village of Rathmullan, on the shore of Lough Swilly, Co. Donegal, accompanied by ninety loyal followers.

It was in exile, in Rome, that the famed Hugh O'Neill died in 1616 at the age of 66.

The O'Neills were also at the forefront of what are known as the Irish Confederate Wars, or The Wars of the Three Kingdoms – a bloody conflagration sparked through the harsh policy of plantation and restrictions on the civil rights of Catholics.

England had its own distractions with the Civil War that culminated in the execution of Charles I in 1649, and from 1641 to 1649 Ireland was ruled by a rebel group known as the Irish Catholic Confederation, or the Confederation of Kilkenny.

Among the confederation's leaders were Hugh Dubh O'Neill, or 'Black Hugh', 5th Earl of Tyrone, his uncle Owen Roe O'Neill and their kinsman Sir Phelim O'Neill.

For his role in the Confederate Wars, Sir Phelim was hanged, drawn and quartered for treason in Dublin in February of 1653 after being captured at Roughan Castle, in Co. Tyrone.

This was four years after the execution of Charles I and the invasion of Ireland by England's Oliver Cromwell.

The Lord Protector, as he was known, had the three main aims of quashing all forms of rebellion, the 'removal' of all Catholic landowners who had taken part in the rebellion, and the conversion of the native Irish to the Protestant faith.

Under the 1652 Cromwellian Act for the Settlement of

Ireland, Sir Phelim had been named as one of the ringleaders of the rebellion that had broken out eleven years earlier.

His kinsman, Owen Roe O'Neill, or 'Red Owen', a nephew of the 2nd Earl of Tyrone, was the professional soldier who also fought with distinction in the Confederate Wars right up until his death in Clough Oughter Castle in 1649 at the age of 59.

His nephew, Hugh Dubh O'Neill, 5th Earl of Tyrone, was also a professional soldier who commanded the defenders during the siege from 1650 to 1651 of Limerick by Cromwell's Parliamentary forces.

Later captured and only narrowly escaping execution, he was imprisoned for a time in the grim confines of the Tower of London before he was released and allowed to go into exile in Spain, where he died in 1660 at the age of 49.

In later centuries, bearers of the O'Neill name have gained distinction in lands far from the original homeland of their ancestors.

Born in 1828 to Irish parents who had settled in Glasgow, Scotland, Charles O'Neill immigrated to New Zealand and later Australia.

An engineer, politician and philanthropist, he represented New Zealand's Otago region in parliament from 1886 to 1870 before settling in Australia and becoming one of the co-founders, before his death in 1900, of the international Roman Catholic charitable organisation, the St Vincent de Paul Society.

Back in Ireland, bearers of the O'Neill name have attained high political office and honours.

Becoming the 2nd Viscount O'Neill after the death of his father in 1798 and 1st Earl O'Neill following the Act of Union between Ireland and England in 1800, Charles O'Neill was of the O'Neills of Shane's Castle, in Co. Antrim; born in 1799, the earldom became extinct on his death in 1841.

Also of the O'Neills of Shane's Castle was Captain Arthur O'Neill, the Ulster Unionist Member (MP) of the United Kingdom Parliament for Antrim Mid.

Killed in action in November of 1914 at the age of 38, he has the dubious distinction of having been the first MP to be lost during the First World War.

His son, Terence O'Neill, Baron O'Neill of The Maine, was the Ulster Unionist politician who from 1963 to 1969 served as the 4th Prime Minister of Northern Ireland; born in the year of his father's death in 1914, he died in 1990.

In the top levels of international diplomacy, Sir Con O'Neill, born in 1912 and who died in 1988, was the leading British civil servant and diplomat who, in the 1970s, headed the team that negotiated the United Kingdom's entry into the European Economic Community.

Across the ocean to the United States, Thomas O'Neill, Jr. was the politician recognised as having been one of America's most influential liberal Democrats of the twentieth century.

Better known as Tip O'Neill – a nickname he was given in honour of the baseball player of that name – he was born to parents of Irish stock in Cambridge, Massachusetts, in 1912.

A keen baseball player in his youth and captain of his school baseball team, he later went on to serve in the U.S. House of Representatives for 34 years, representing Congressional districts in his native Massachusetts.

Speaker of the House from 1977 until his retirement from politics in 1987, he became the second longest-serving Speaker in U.S. political history.

O'Neill, whose tenure as Speaker embraced the presidencies of Gerald Ford, Jimmy Carter and Ronald Reagan, was presented with the Presidential Medal of Freedom three years before his death in 1994.

Away from the often cut-throat world of politics, bearers of the O'Neill name and its spelling variants such as O'Neil and Neill have achieved distinction in a wide range of much different pursuits.

Chapter four:
On the world stage

Not only a film and television screenwriter and novelist, Charles O'Neal was also the first in a family dynasty of show business O'Neals.

Born in 1904 in Raeford, North Carolina, he worked for a time in an acting troupe along with his wife, Patricia Callaghan, before turning his talents to writing.

His screenwriting credits include a number of B-movies such as *Cry of the Werewolf* and *Seventh Victim*, while he also scripted episodes of the television series *The Untouchables*.

His 1949 novel *Three Wishes for Jamie McRuin* was later adapted for the 1952 stage musical *Three Wishes for Jamie*.

O'Neal, who died in 1996, was the father of the actor **Ryan O'Neal**, born in Los Angeles in 1941.

First coming to prominence in the television series *Peyton Place*, from 1964 until 1966, his first film success was the 1970 *Love Story*, for which he received an Academy Award nomination for Best Actor.

Further films have included the 1972 *What's Up, Doc?* the 1973 *Paper Moon* and, from 1984, *The Irreconcilable*, while from 2007 until 2010 he starred in the American television series *Bones*.

Married from 1963 until 1967 to Joanna Moore and

from 1967 to 1973 to Leigh Taylor-Young, his partner for a number of years afterwards was the actress Farah Fawcett, until her death in 2009.

His daughter is the actress **Tatum O'Neal**, born in Los Angeles in 1963 and who, at the time of writing, is the youngest actress to have won an Academy Award.

The award, for Best Supporting Actress, came at the tender age of ten for her starring role beside her father in *Paper Moon*, while she also starred beside him in the 1976 *Nickelodeon*.

Married to the American tennis star John McEnroe from 1986 until the couple divorced in 1994, she has also starred in films that include the 1976 *The Bad News Bears* and, from 1996, *Basquiat*, while she has also appeared on American television series that include *Sex and the City*.

Still keeping acting in the family, her brother, **Griffin O'Neal**, born in Los Angeles in 1964, has appeared in films that include *April Fool's Day* and *Ghoulies III*.

Best known for his role as Al Bundy in the 1987-1997 television sitcom *Married with Children* – for which he won two separate Golden Globe Award nominations for Best Performance by an Actor in a TV-Series-Comedy – **Ed O'Neill** is the American actor who was born in 1946 in Youngstown, Ohio.

Film roles include the 1991 *Dutch* and the 1999 *The Bone Collector*, while at the time of writing he stars in the U.S. sitcom *Modern Family*.

Still on the stage, **Amy O'Neill**, born in 1971 in Pacific Palisades, California, is the American actress whose film credits include the 1989 Disney film *Honey, I Shrunk the Kids*, for which she was nominated for an Academy Young Actress Award, while **Robert O'Neill**, born in 1966 in Weston-super-Mare, is a British actor of Irish roots.

In 1988 he won the Laurence Olivier Theatre Award for Best Actor in a Musical for his performance in *Blood Brothers*.

An actor of stage, film and television, **Dick O'Neill** was the American actor who was born in New York City in 1928 and died in 1998.

His film roles include *The Taking of Pelham 123* and *Prizzi's Honor*, but he is best known for his role as Charlie Cagney in the television police series *Cagney and Lacey*.

Born in 1973, **Willa O'Neill** is the New Zealand actress known for her role as Althea in the television series *Hercules: The Legendary Journeys* and as Lila in *Xena: Warrior Princess*.

Born in 1962 in Buckinghamshire, **Maggie O'Neill** is the English actress whose film credits include the 1986 *Mona Lisa* and whose British television credits include *Peak Practice* and *Shameless*, while Nigel Neill is the actor better known as **Sam Neill**.

Born in 1947 in Omagh, Northern Ireland, he immigrated with his family to New Zealand at the age of seven, and has enjoyed international success with films that include the 1990 *The Hunt for Red October*, the 1993

Jurassic Park and its sequel *Jurassic Park II* and, from 2010, *Daybreakers*.

Bearers of the O'Neill name have also excelled, and continue to excel, in the highly competitive world of sport.

On the fields of European football, **Martin O'Neill** is the manager and former top midfield player who was born in 1952 in Kilrea, Northern Ireland.

His playing career began in Ireland, playing with Derry City as a youth and later with Lisburn Distillery, before moving to England where he played from 1971 to 1981 with the European Cup-winning Nottingham Forest.

Also captain of the Northern Ireland national team for a time, he later managed clubs that include Leicester City and, from 2000 to 2005, Scottish Premier League club Celtic – leading the club to the 2003 UEFA Cup Final and to three Scottish Premier League titles.

Appointed manager of English club Aston Villa in 2006, he resigned from the post in August 2010.

From football to baseball, James Edward O'Neill was the Canadian left fielder better known as **Tip O'Neill**.

Born in 1858 in Springfield, Ontario, he became a baseball legend between 1883 and 1892 playing for teams that included the New York Gothams, St Louis Browns and Cincinnati Reds; he died in 1915.

Born in Philadelphia in 1917, **Harry O'Neill** was the professional baseball catcher who played for the Philadelphia Athletics.

A Marine Corps lieutenant with the 40th Marine Division, he was killed by a Japanese sniper during the battle of Iwo Jima in March of 1945 – one of the two Major League Baseball players, along with Elmer Gedeon, to be killed in action during the Second World War.

In the Canadian national sport of ice hockey, **Brian O'Neill** is a former executive of the National Hockey League; born in Montreal in 1929, he was elected to the Hockey Hall of Fame in 1994.

On a musical note, **Damian O'Neill**, born in 1961 in Belfast, is the lead guitarist with the Northern Irish pop/punk band The Undertones, while his older brother, **John O'Neill**, born in 1957 is the band's rhythm guitarist.

In a different musical genre, **Dennis O'Neill**, born in 1948, is the acclaimed Welsh operatic tenor who in 2007 was appointed director of the Cardiff International Academy of Voice.

From opera to rhythm and blues, **Alexander O'Neill**, born in 1953 in Natchez, Mississippi, is the recording artist whose hit songs include *Saturday Love* and *Never Knew Love Like This*.

Bearers of the O'Neill name have also made their mark on the world of literature – particularly the great American playwright **Eugene O'Neill**.

Born in New York City in 1888 of Irish extraction, he battled for a number of years with alcoholism and depression before achieving success with his play *Beyond the Horizon*, which opened on Broadway in 1920 and gained him a Pulitzer Prize – as did his 1922 *Anna Christie*.

Further plays included his 1924 *Desire under the Elms* and his 1931 *Mourning Becomes Electra*, while in 1936 he received the Nobel Prize for Literature.

It was not until three years after his death in 1953 that his autobiographical *Long Day's Journey Into Night* was published, posthumously winning him a Pulitzer Prize in 1957.

Portrayed by Jack Nicholson in the 1981 film *Reds*, concerning the life and times of his friend and contemporary John Reed, founder of the Communist Labor Party of America, O'Neill was the father of **Oona O'Neill**.

Born in Bermuda in 1925, she was disowned by her disapproving father when, at the age of 18, she married the English actor and film director Charlie Chaplin, who was 36 years her senior.

Father and daughter never spoke again, but she and Chaplin enjoyed 35 happy years of marriage and she took the title of Lady Chaplin when her husband was knighted.

She died in 1991 and was the mother of eight children, including the actress Geraldine Chaplin.

Born in 1938, **Gene O'Neill** is the best-selling American science fiction, horror and fantasy author whose *Taste of Tenderloin* won him the 2010 Bram Stoker Award for Best Fiction Collection, while **James O'Neill** is an acclaimed Irish author.

Born in 1962 in Dún Laoghaire, his novels include the 1989 *Disturbance*, his 1990 *Kilbrack* and, from 2001, *At Swim, Two Boys*.

From the world of books to the equally creative world of art, **Dan O'Neill**, born in Belfast in 1920, was the largely self-taught Northern Irish artist whose Romantic paintings include his 1949 *Place du Tertre* and, from 1951, *Western Landscape*; he died in 1974.

In a different artistic genre, William Neill, born in 1911 in Partick, Glasgow was the Scottish cartoonist better known as **Bud Neill**.

Drawing cartoon strips for a number of Glasgow-based newspapers between the 1940s and the 1960s, particularly the *Glasgow Evening Times* and the *Sunday Mail*, he is best known for his humorous *Sheriff Lobey Dosser of Calton Creek* strips; he died in 1970.

One of the most colourful bearers of the O'Neill name was William O'Neill, better known as **Buckey O'Neill** – a nickname derived from his habit of 'bucking the tiger', or playing contrary to the odds, in card games.

Born in 1860, by the age of 20 he had settled in Tombstone, Arizona. As a reporter with the *Tombstone Epitaph* newspaper, he became acquainted with such figures as Wyatt Earp and members of the notorious Clanton and McLaury gangs of rustlers and murderers.

War between the rival gangs reached its climax on October 26th, 1881, with the infamous Gunfight at the O.K.

Corral – and O'Neill was the first newspaperman to report on it.

Quitting Tombstone for Prescott, Arizona, and supplementing his income by gambling and occasional gold mining ventures, he worked as a court reporter before founding the *Hoof and Horn* newspaper for the livestock industry.

Following the outbreak of war between the United States and Spain in 1898, the adventurous O'Neill joined the voluntary militia known as the Rough Riders, becoming captain of Troop A.

On July 1st 1898, in action at Kettle Hill, near the village of Santiago de Cuba, in Cuba, he had been strolling up and down in full view of the enemy, nonchalantly smoking a cigarette, when he was shot dead by a sniper.

Seconds before he had been hit, he had laughed off desperate appeals from his comrades to take cover, uttering the famous last words: "The Spanish bullet isn't made that will kill me!"

Key dates in Ireland's history from the first settlers to the formation of the Irish Republic:

circa 7000 B.C.	Arrival and settlement of Stone Age people.
circa 3000 B.C.	Arrival of settlers of New Stone Age period.
circa 600 B.C.	First arrival of the Celts.
200 A.D.	Establishment of Hill of Tara, Co. Meath, as seat of the High Kings.
circa 432 A.D.	Christian mission of St. Patrick.
800-920 A.D.	Invasion and subsequent settlement of Vikings.
1002 A.D.	Brian Boru recognised as High King.
1014	Brian Boru killed at battle of Clontarf.
1169-1170	Cambro-Norman invasion of the island.
1171	Henry II claims Ireland for the English Crown.
1366	Statutes of Kilkenny ban marriage between native Irish and English.
1529-1536	England's Henry VIII embarks on religious Reformation.
1536	Earl of Kildare rebels against the Crown.
1541	Henry VIII declared King of Ireland.
1558	Accession to English throne of Elizabeth I.
1565	Battle of Affane.
1569-1573	First Desmond Rebellion.
1579-1583	Second Desmond Rebellion.
1594-1603	Nine Years War.
1606	Plantation' of Scottish and English settlers.
1607	Flight of the Earls.
1632-1636	Annals of the Four Masters compiled.
1641	Rebellion over policy of plantation and other grievances.
1649	Beginning of Cromwellian conquest.
1688	Flight into exile in France of Catholic Stuart monarch James II as Protestant Prince William of Orange invited to take throne of England along with his wife, Mary.
1689	William and Mary enthroned as joint monarchs; siege of Derry.
1690	Jacobite forces of James defeated by William at battle of the Boyne (July) and Dublin taken.

1691	Athlone taken by William; Jacobite defeats follow at Aughrim, Galway, and Limerick; conflict ends with Treaty of Limerick (October) and Irish officers allowed to leave for France.
1695	Penal laws introduced to restrict rights of Catholics; banishment of Catholic clergy.
1704	Laws introduced constricting rights of Catholics in landholding and public office.
1728	Franchise removed from Catholics.
1791	Foundation of United Irishmen republican movement.
1796	French invasion force lands in Bantry Bay.
1798	Defeat of Rising in Wexford and death of United Irishmen leaders Wolfe Tone and Lord Edward Fitzgerald.
1800	Act of Union between England and Ireland.
1803	Dublin Rising under Robert Emmet.
1829	Catholics allowed to sit in Parliament.
1845-1849	The Great Hunger: thousands starve to death as potato crop fails and thousands more emigrate.
1856	Phoenix Society founded.
1858	Irish Republican Brotherhood established.
1873	Foundation of Home Rule League.
1893	Foundation of Gaelic League.
1904	Foundation of Irish Reform Association.
1913	Dublin strikes and lockout.
1916	Easter Rising in Dublin and proclamation of an Irish Republic.
1917	Irish Parliament formed after Sinn Fein election victory.
1919-1921	War between Irish Republican Army and British Army.
1922	Irish Free State founded, while six northern counties remain part of United Kingdom as Northern Ireland, or Ulster; civil war up until 1923 between rival republican groups.
1949	Foundation of Irish Republic after all remaining constitutional links with Britain are severed.